The Byzantine Empire and the Plague: The [ ] Pandemic that Ravaged the Byzantines in [ ]

By Charles River Editors

Josse Lieferinxe's painting of St. Sebastian pleading with Jesus for the life of a gravedigger affected by the Plague of Justinian

About Charles River Editors

Charles River Editors provides superior editing and original writing services across the digital publishing industry, with the expertise to create digital content for publishers across a vast range of subject matter. In addition to providing original digital content for third party publishers, we also republish civilization's greatest literary works, bringing them to new generations of readers via ebooks.

Sign up here to receive updates about free books as we publish them, and visit Our Kindle Author Page to browse today's free promotions and our most recently published Kindle titles.

Introduction

Carol Raddato's picture of the partially built basilica in Philippi, which remained unfinished because of the Plague of Justinian

"[Theodore] made very large pits, inside each of which 70,000 corpses were laid down. He thus appointed men there, who brought down corpses, sorted them and piled them up. They pressed them in rows on top of each other, in the same way as someone presses hay in a loft ... Men and women were trodden down, and in the little space between them the young and infants were pressed down, trodden with the feet and trampled down like spoilt grapes." - John of Ephesus

The Bubonic Plague was the worst affliction ever visited upon Europe and the Mediterranean world. Within a few short years, a quarter of the population was taken after a short but torturous illness. Those who escaped faced famine and economic hardship, crops were left unsown; harvests spoiled for lack of harvesters, and villages, towns, and great cities were depopulated. Markets were destroyed, and trade ground to a halt. It must have seemed like the end of the world to the terrified populace. The horror abated, only to return years later, often with less virulence but no less misery.

Many who read a description of that plague might immediately think of the Black Death, the great epidemic that ravaged Europe and the Middle East from 1347-1351, but it actually refers to the lesser-known but arguably worse Plague of Justinian that descended upon the Mediterranean world in 541 and continued to decimate it over the next 200 years. The effects of the pestilence on history was every bit as dramatic as the one in the Late Middle Ages. In fact, the case could be made that the Plague of Justinian was a major factor in the molding of Europe and, consequently, the rest of the world as it is known today, marking a monumental crossroad between the ancient and medieval worlds.

The Byzantine Empire and the Plague: The History and Legacy of the Pandemic that Ravaged the Byzantines in the Early Middle Ages charts the history of the pestilence over the course of two centuries and how it shaped subsequent events, bringing down nations while inadvertently lifting others. It also describes the diseases' victims, and how certain segments of society may have avoided contracting it. Along with pictures depicting important people, places, and events, you will learn about the Byzantine Empire and the plague like never before.

An Outbreak

In 541 CE, Constantinople was one of the most advanced cities in the world. It boasted a population of 500,000[1] and was looked upon by the inhabitants of Europe, North Africa, Asia Minor, and the Levant as the capital of the civilized world. In 324, Emperor Constantine I had transferred the seat of the Roman Empire from Rome to a city on the Bosporus named Byzantium, renaming it after himself. About 150 years later, the Western Roman Empire succumbed to barbarian invasions, but in the east, the emperors continued to rule from Constantinople, and though the successor of the Eastern Roman Empire is now widely known as the Byzantine Empire, the emperors continued to consider it the Roman Empire.

Justinian I, now known as Justinian the Great, was the emperor at the time. When he took the throne, Persian power was growing under the talented Khurso, which threatened Byzantium. On top of that, less settled peoples such as the Huns, Avars, Turks, and Slavs presented problems and could be used by the Persians as an advance guard against the Byzantines. Justinian bought off the Persians, the perennial enemies of the Greeks, so he could turn his attention west. That arguably turned out to be a geopolitical mistake since it was impossible to keep the former Western Roman Empire under control, and later emperors eventually developed a series of treaties and alliances that demanded the recognition of the emperor as the supreme authority but did not require direct rule. At the very least, the main threat to the empire lay in the east, so the territory to the west should have been left to develop itself under the indirect rule of the Byzantines.

---

[1] Harl 2015

A contemporary mosaic depicting Justinian I

That was easier said than done, however, because Justinian's focus to the west was a result of the fact that Roman authority had collapsed there only about 50 years earlier, and the fall of the Western half of the empire meant that trade opportunities were lost, Roman cities fell into disrepair, and what was once a unified empire was now an unsettled patchwork of tribes and ethnicities. Justinian would spend a huge amount of manpower and money to reunify the two halves of Rome.

Over the course of nearly 40 years in power, Justinian the Great succeeded in reversing the empire's declining fortunes, and his top general, Belisarius, defeated the Persians and reconquered North Africa and Italy from the barbarians. At home, he accomplished the monumental work of codifying Roman law, providing a legal framework with which to unite his empire. He built the Hagia Sophia, the Church of Holy Wisdom in Constantinople, which was dedicated in 537 after five years of labor. Its golden dome was surmounted by a great cross, rising 55 meters from its foundations. At 82 meters long and 73 meters wide, the cross was adorned with the finest gold, marble, and stone the empire could provide. The most gifted artisans were summoned to fashion exquisite mosaics depicting Jesus Christ, his mother, and the saints, as well as the great emperors of Constantinople. Hagia Sophia continues to be a wonder of the Christian world, a monument not only to the greatness of the empire but to Justinian's grandeur. Procopius, a historian who was no admirer of Justinian and his accomplishments, still felt compelled to write:

> "[The church] is distinguished by indescribable beauty, excelling both in its size…and in the harmony of its measures, having no part excessive and none deficient; being more magnificent than ordinary buildings, and much more elegant than those which are not of so just a proportion. The church is singularly full of light and sunshine; you would declare that the place is not lighted by the sun from without, but that the rays are produced within itself, such an abundance of light is poured into this church…

> "Now above the arches is raised a circular building of a curved form through which the light of day first shines; for the building, which I imagine overtops the whole country, has small openings left on purpose, so that the places where these intervals occur may serve for the light to come through. Thus far I imagine the building is not incapable of being described, even by a weak and feeble tongue. As the arches are arranged in a quadrangular figure, the stone-work between them takes the shape of a triangle, the lower angle of each triangle, being compressed where the arches unite, is slender, while the upper part becomes wider as it rises in the space between them, and ends against the circle which rests upon them, forming there its remaining angles. A spherical-shaped dome standing upon this circle makes it exceedingly beautiful; from the lightness of the building, it does not appear to rest upon a solid foundation, but to cover the place beneath as though it were suspended from heaven by the fabled golden chain. All these parts surprisingly joined to one another in the air, suspended one from another, and resting only on that which is next to them, form the work into one admirably harmonious whole, which spectators do not dwell upon for long in the mass, as each individual part attracts the eye to itself.

> "No one ever became weary of this spectacle, but those who are in the church delight in what they see, and, when they leave, magnify it in their talk. Moreover it is impossible accurately to describe the gold, and silver, and gems, presented [to]…Emperor Justinian, but by the description of one part, I leave the rest to be inferred. That part of the church which is especially sacred, and where the priests alone are allowed to enter, which is called the Sanctuary, contains forty thousand pounds' weight of silver."[2]

---

[2] Procopius 1894

Arild Vågen's 2013 photo of the Hagia Sophia

The Hagia Sophia and other projects were paid for by the enormous wealth pouring into Constantinople, for the city, poised as it was between Europe and Asia, was the premiere trading center of the Western world. From Africa came gold, ivory, spices, and corn; from Italy, iron and timber; and from the lands of the Franks (France and Western Germany), wine and beer. The Khazars of the Eurasian Steppes brought furs, and from China came rich fabrics and spices via the Silk Road passing through Persia. Constantinople and its emperor were at the height of their glory.

The manner in which the economy functioned at home and the various trade networks that brought people to and from Constantinople would play a major role in the spread of the plague. Restoring a centralized state in Byzantium was paramount in all respects, but of course, economic policy and landholding were the main sources of revenue. Slaves, serfs and tenants were legally defined classes, and, given the nature of the law in the East, the older patrimonial model of monarchy did not exist. Private property apart from the emperor was protected.

In and around Constantinople, slave and serf labor still functioned as a vestigial remnant of ancient Rome. The use of slave gangs (often consisting of prisoners of war) intensified small-scale farming in the hinterlands, but since slaves work only to the extent necessary to avoid punishment, slave labor typically had poor standards, especially compared to serf labor.

The 6th century brought an increase in the rate of serfdom among the rural population. These were mostly from regions of barbaric groups having colonial status. As historian Peter Saris noted, "The late fifth century and, in particular, the reign of the Emperor Anastasius (r. 491–518) was clearly associated with a major consolidation of aristocratic power at the grassroots of early Byzantine society. Through the development of the offices of *pagarch* and *vindex*, magnate households tightened their control over the administrative and fiscal structures of provincial life." (Saris, 2006: 200). This was the reality that Justinian later saw as irrational, and from this, the 6th century drive to dispossess small landholders and even free peasant homesteads makes more sense. Draconian punishments were increasingly the norm for dispossessing elites of their lands too; according to the new legal code of Justinian, lands without heir, abandoned lands or lands confiscated from political opponents went to Justinian and the state. In practice, this meant that loyal landlords were favored and were, as a result, given a great degree of judicial freedom on the manor. Even the property rights of serfs were not decreed inviolable (as no property was ever inviolable in Byzantium); what truly mattered was the political stance of the lord.

A free "serf" in this context was a bit like a yeoman farmer. He was independent in the sense that he had a clear title of ownership, but other than that, the serf was essentially a renter with few rights. Slowly, this class became more dominant in Byzantium during and after the reign of Justinian, but the level of freedom it enjoyed was directly proportional to the strength of the emperor (Saris, 2006: 70-76).

While the era just prior to Justinian was a time of consolidation, this should not obscure the reality of many medium and small landlords throughout the empire. Growth was clearly visible in the major cities and the urban economy, which largely contributed to the resilience and stability of the Byzantine currency and basic confidence. The city housed the bulk of slaveholders and many of the slaves. Slave labor was used in certain crafts and municipal work (Saris, 2006: 125), and artisans and traders developed a guild system which was quite unlike the western variant. The guild was a taxpaying unit and was state controlled. It provided a certain minimum, especially a place in the relevant district of the city. Gold and silversmiths acted as a "central bank" in the early part of the 6th century, acting as loan-sharks and usurers.

In the year 536, a dreadful omen descended over Europe when a dark veil fell upon the sun. While Earth was not completely plunged into darkness, the lack of sunlight caused temperatures to drop and crops to fail. There was snow in summer, and millions died of starvation and cold. This bizarre phenomenon lasted three years and affected not just Europe, but the whole northern hemisphere. Experts postulate it was caused by volcanic dust, possibly from an eruption of Krakatoa,[3] but regardless of how it happened, it initiated a miniature ice age, and while there was certainly a scientific explanation, most medieval people viewed it as a sign of impending doom and the wrath of God. Indeed, the cooler temperatures and wetter summers would have encouraged an increase in the rat population, and rats carried fleas bearing deadly bacteria.

Around the end of spring in 541, a merchant ship from Pelusim in the Nile Delta sailed into the

---

[3] Wohletz 2000

Golden Horn (the inlet between Constantinople and the suburb of Galata) from the Sea of Marmara and docked in the harbor, where the walls of the city extended into the sea. The ship was carrying corn, upon which Constantinople's massive population and people in the empire's other large cities depended. When the ship arrived, some of the seamen on board were ill and exhibiting unusual symptoms, such as painful swelling of the neck, armpits, or groin. They also complained of high fevers and muscle cramps. Much to the horror of onlookers, some vomited blood, while the flesh of others' extremities had turned black. In time, horrible swelling resembling massive boils began to break, with pus and blood pouring out. The affected sailors died within a few days.

Within a week, further outbreaks of the horrific disease occurred, first among merchants, sailors, and dock laborers. After that, it appeared among the general population, and since it seemed to affect beggars, bishops, finely-robed noblemen, and women equally, it seemed that no gender or class would be spared.

The climate around the time of the outbreak was marked by below-average temperatures, damaging crops and causing famine. This meant that people would have migrated throughout the empire in search of food and better agricultural land. It would have also meant an increased reliance on grain imports from Egypt, both of which were favourable to the rapid spread of the pestilence.

Once infected, a victim had but a few days to live. Some might survive a week, but only a very few recovered entirely. The plague was not selective; the hale and hearty, along with the frail and weak, were struck suddenly down with the slimmest of chance for survival. People, as well as livestock, were affected by the disease.

Soon, the plague spread to major trading cities in the eastern Mediterranean, including Antioch and Alexandria. From there, it spread through North Africa, the Balkans, Italy, and Spain. It infected Francia (the kingdom of the Franks), the British Isles, Germany, the Eurasian Steppes, and Persia, following trade routes and inexorably following populations fleeing the pestilence. Provincial trade routes connected with the coast, inland towns, and rural regions were not spared. Bishop John of Ephesus (ca. 507-588) personified the plague when he wrote,

> When this plague was passing from one land to another, many people saw shapes of bronze boats and [figures] sitting in them resembling people with their heads cut off. Holding staves, also of bronze, they moved along on the sea and could be seen going whithersoever they headed. These figures were seen everywhere in a frightening fashion, especially at night. Like flashing bronze and like fire did they appear, black people without heads sitting in a glistening boat and travelling swiftly on the sea, so that this sight almost caused the souls of the people who saw it to expire.[4]

---

[4] Rosen 2008:222

Bishop Gregory of Tours recorded that in Clermont (Francia), as many as six victims were buried in the same grave due to the lack of coffins, and in Constantinople, new cemeteries had to be built across the Golden Horn. The leaders of the Church would not countenance cremation, believed contrary to the dignity of a body that might be resurrected on the last day. Rather than succumb to a death marked with bloody vomiting and terrible agony, many citizens of the city climbed the great walls and threw themselves from the parapets into the sea. At its height, the pestilence killed around 5,000 people in Constantinople per day.[5]

Symptoms, Causes, and Treatment

"For the rest, so that the conditions, causes and symptoms of this pestilential disease should be made plain to all, I have decided to set them out in writing. Those of both sees who were in health, and in no fear of death, were struck by four savage blows to the flesh. First, out of the blue, a kind of chilly stiffness troubled their bodies. They felt a tingling sensation, as if they were being pricked by the points of arrows. The next stage was a fearsome attack which took the form of an extremely hard, solid boil. In some people this developed under the armpit and in other in the groin between the scrotum and the body. As it grew more solid, its burning heat caused the patients to fall into an acute and putrid fever, with severe headaches. As it intensified its extreme bitterness could have various effects. In some cases it gave rise to an intolerable stench. In others it brought vomiting of blood, or swellings near the place from which the corrupt humor arose; on the back, across the chest, near the thigh. Some people lay as if in a drunken stupor and could not be roused." - Gabriele Mussis

Based on the symptoms, physicians and historians believe that Justinian's Constantinople had been introduced to Bubonic Plague, the same horrific malady that would later be referred to as the Black Death when it struck Europe in the 14th century. Caused by the bacterium *Yersinia pestis,* it is transmitted by fleas on rats and came from the Orient. DNA samples of inert bacterium taken from a victim in Germany indicates that the 541 strain originated somewhere in the Tian Shan Mountains of Central Asia.[6] The Silk Road, the major trading route between Europe and Asia, passed through these ranges, so the strain carried by those sailors in Constantinople had infected Egypt through trade with Ethiopia, which was in touch with merchants from the East.

---

[5] Mango 1980
[6] Eroshenko 2017

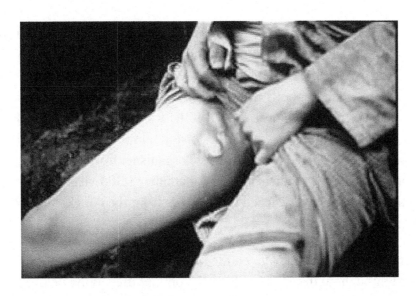

A victim of the Bubonic Plague with swollen lymph nodes visible

A victim of the Bubonic Plague with fingers blackened by the illness

Galen's advice concerning epidemics was the best and simplest: "Leave quickly, go far away, return slowly."[7] However, most of the threatened population could not flee, and those who did found that the pestilence usually followed anyway. Meanwhile, Byzantine physicians were unfamiliar with the symptoms and thus utterly helpless to deal with the disease. There had been

---

[7] "The Black Death" 2020

epidemics in the Roman world before, most notably from the years 165-180, during which 5,000,000 people were killed by something resembling smallpox or measles. A similar blight struck in 249 and lasted 13 years, but a plague marked by swelling (technically called buboes, hence the name Bubonic Plague), boils full of blood and pus, and the rapid onset of gangrene, agony, and fever was previously unknown. Even if the Roman physicians had known of it, there would have been virtually nothing they could do to stop its spread or cure it. The concept of diseases being caused by the spread of microscopic organisms from person to person simply did not exist and would not become medical dogma for another 1,300 years. Until then, it was widely believed that pestilence was caused by *miasma* (from the Greek "pollution"), poisonous air emanating from decaying matter.

There was a certain logic to the idea given the limited knowledge of physicians, and it was generally accepted throughout the world. After all, communities living near rotting waste seemed to be heavily afflicted with the disease, and soldiers on battlefields in proximity to rotting corpses often became ill. The Greek physician Hippocrates (ca. 460-377 BCE) and the Roman physician Galen (129-ca. 216) were considered unchallengeable authorities on medicine, and they had been avid proponents of the miasma theory. While it turned out they were wrong, their theories were certainly improvements on the superstitious notion that disease was caused by vengeful gods or demons. Furthermore, the method of preventing disease based on the *miasma* theory corresponds in large part to modern notions of hygiene in that decaying matter had to be removed from areas of habitation. As a result, the bodies of plague victims were carted away, buried in deep pits, and their clothing and belongings were burned, which was useful in preventing the plague from spreading even further.

At the same time, other notions of prevention shared nothing with modern medicine. Based on the belief that foul odors indicated the presence of miasma, the air was frequently "purified" with sweet-smelling perfumes, spices, and unguents. Naturally, these did little to ward off the plague, though the notion that incense and unguents cleanse the air remains widespread to this day.

To treat the symptoms, physicians turned to Hippocrates's theory of the humors, which was perpetuated by Galen. The theory held that the body possessed four fluids, or humors, which corresponded to the four elements from which all material being was composed: earth (black bile), fire (yellow bile), water (phlegm), and air (water). A predominance of one humor affected an individual's temperament, so a warm, happy, extroverted personality was associated with blood. A choleric, fiery temperament indicated a predominance of yellow bile (*khole* in Greek), while a melancholic or dark disposition was caused by the predominance of black bile. Finally, a phlegmatic temperament was due to an excess of phlegm.

It was believed that an individual in good health enjoyed a balance of the four humors and that illness was an expression of imbalance. Galen expounded upon Hippocrates's theory by teaching that excess humors needed expelling from the body, typically via bloodletting, vomiting, sneezing, or urination. Galen also believed that diet might also address an imbalance.

Thus, when blood, which was believed to be stagnant in the body, would swell to excess, physicians would lance or stab boils to release it. Fevers might be treated by chilling the body or warming it, for Galen believed symptoms could be treated with their opposites or similarities. Needless to say, these treatments were not effective, but that didn't stop the Western world from using techniques like bloodletting for another 1,300 years, if only because physicians figured (often incorrectly) that trying something was better than doing nothing.

There were obvious deficiencies in Roman medical theory, but these problems were by no means confined to the Greco-Roman world, given that the state of medicine in the Roman Empire was advanced for its time. At first, state hospitals existed for the military and state slaves but not the general public, who were served by the hospitals attached to churches. By the 6th century, however, Byzantine emperors began constructing hospitals for the public alongside those run by the Church.

There were three general grades of physicians: court, public, and private. The physicians of the imperial court were almost always aristocrats, usually given the title of count. Public physicians, employed by the city, were required by law to "honestly attend the poor, rather than basely...serve the rich."[8] Private practitioners were regarded as the worst in the medical profession, for it was widely assumed they treated sick people for material gain alone. The finest physicians in the empire were trained in the famous Medical School of Alexandria, which had been founded in 331 BCE. This was somewhat ironic given that the plague came to Constantinople from Egypt.

The largest hospital in Constantinople was named after St. Pantaleon, a physician and martyr of the 4th century, and as was the case with all hospitals, it filled up quickly. In response to the outbreak, Emperor Justinian canceled subsidies for public doctors and transferred them to the hospitals, which in essence was a form of public healthcare, at least in Constantinople and important urban centers during the plague. Rural inhabitants and the very poor were forced to resort to alternate forms of succor, usually prayers and superstitions. Sufferers sought the touch of the relic of a holy man or woman, and the Church possessed a ceremony for the sick, the *euchelaeon,* whereby the subject was anointed with oil and prayed over. Many reverted to the practices of their pagan ancestors by using charms and amulets. It was probably little consolation for these victims to discover the remedies were about as effective as the expensive "cures" that were purchased from doctors by the rich and powerful.

To be fair to those in and around Constantinople, Europeans wouldn't fare much better when the Bubonic Plague struck again 900 years later. Due to their limited knowledge of medicine, and the almost total lack of any reliable method of studying and treating disease, there were no

---

[8] Rosen 2008:211

verifiable ways known to avoid contracting the disease. As such, rumors began to spread abundantly. When the Bubonic Plague hit Europe in the 14th century, Louis Heyligen, a musician serving Cardinal Giovanni Colonna in Italy, hoped that maybe he had learned something while working in the papal court that could save his friends. In a letter, he wrote, "I am writing to you, most dearly beloved, so that you should know in what perils we are now living. And if you wish to preserve yourselves, the best advice is that a man should eat and drink moderately, and avoid getting cold, and refrain from any excess, and above all mix little with people—unless it be with a few who have healthy breath; but it is best to stay at home until the epidemic has passed. According to astrologers the epidemic takes ten years to complete its cycle, of which three have now elapsed, and so it is to be feared that in the end it will have encircled the whole world, although they say that it will affect the cold region more slowly."

   On the other hand, Giovanni Boccaccio had his own ideas about what would prevent one from catching the plague, though since he was neither a doctor nor a scientist, his ideas were more of a hopeful collection of rumors going around than any sort of definitive advice. He wrote, "Some thought that moderate living and the avoidance of all superfluity would preserve them from the epidemic. They formed small communities, living entirely separate from everybody else. They shut themselves up in houses where there were no sick, eating the finest food and drinking the best wine very temperately, avoiding all excess, allowing no news or discussion of death and sickness, and passing the time in music and suchlike pleasures. Others thought just the opposite. They thought the sure cure for the plague was to drink and be merry, to go about singing and amusing themselves, satisfying every appetite they could, laughing and jesting at what happened. They put their words into practice, spent day and night going from tavern to tavern, drinking immoderately, or went into other people's houses, doing only those things which pleased them. This they could easily do because everyone felt doomed and had abandoned his property, so that most houses became common property and any stranger who went in made use of them as if he had owned them. And with all this bestial behavior, they avoided the sick as much as possible. … Many others adopted a course of life midway between the two just described. They did not restrict their victuals so much as the former, nor allow themselves to be drunken and dissolute like the latter, but satisfied their appetites moderately. They did not shut themselves up, but went about, carrying flowers or scented herbs or perfumes in their hands, in the belief that it was an excellent thing to comfort the brain with such odors; for the whole air was infected with the smell of dead bodies, of sick persons and medicines."

   The flowers or herbs mentioned above were tied together in small bundles called "posies" and may have given rise to a chant later picked up by children. To this day, kids across the world are still familiar with the simple refrain:

"Ring around the rosies

Pocket full of posies

Ashes, ashes

We all fall down."

Although it's impossible to determine with certainty and continues to be debated, many scholars believe the nursery rhyme is a nod to the Black Death. In this seemingly innocuous chant, the first line refers to the bright red cheeks that appeared on the faces of those suffering fever, while the ashes referred to the remains of the burned possessions that had once belonged to the sick. Of course, the dead were the ones who fell down. In support of this interpretation, Peter and Iona Opie, who have long studied nursery rhymes, noted, "The invariable sneezing and falling down in modern English versions have given would-be origin finders the opportunity to say that the rhyme dates back to the Great Plague. A rosy rash, they alleged, was a symptom of the plague, and posies of herbs were carried as protection and to ward off the smell of the disease. Sneezing or coughing was a final fatal symptom, and 'all fall down' was exactly what happened.

While people may have attempted to avoid catching the disease in superstitious but utterly worthless manners, many of those who were well-travelled and well-read in the 14th century noticed that the plague did not seem to manifest itself in the same way everywhere. That may have been because it mutated over time or because there was actually more than one virulent strain going around. The Italian writer Giovanni Boccaccio explained, "The symptoms were not the same as in the East, where a gush of blood from the nose was the plain sign of inevitable death; but it began both in men and women with certain swellings in the groin or under the armpit. They grew to the size of a small apple or an egg, more or less, and were vulgarly called tumors. In a short space of time these tumors spread from the two parts named all over the body. Soon after this the symptoms changed and black or purple spots appeared on the arms or thighs or any other part of the body, sometimes a few large ones, sometimes many little ones. These spots were a certain sign of death, just as the original tumor had been and still remained."

An early 15th century Bible's illustration believed to depict the plague

Other people believed that the disease came from something people ate. Cortusii Patavini Duo recalled, "Also fish are now not generally eaten, men holding that they have been infected by the infected air. Moreover no kinds of spices are eaten or handled, unless they have been in stock for a year, because men are afraid that they might have come from the galleys of which I spoke. For on many occasions eating fresh spices or certain sea fishes had been found to have extremely unpleasant results."

For many, the only cause for the illness, or indeed for any type of misfortune, was the wrath of God, but they still commented on the physical conditions of the victims. A monk known as Agnolo di Tura "the Fat" wrote, "[I]n many places in Siena great pits were dug and piled deep with the multitude of dead ... And there were also those who were so sparsely covered with earth that the dogs dragged them forth and devoured many bodies throughout the city. If I am asked what is the cause of pestilence, what is its physical cause and by what means can someone save himself from it, I answer to the first question that sin is the cause. To the second question, I say that it arises from the sea, as the evangelist says: 'There shall be signs in the sun and in the moon and in the stars; and upon the earth distress of nations, by reason of the confusion of the roaring of the sea and of the waves.' For the devil, by the power committed to him when the seas rise up high, is voiding his poison, sending it forth to be added to the poison in the air, and that air spreads gradually from place to place and enters man through the ears, eyes, nose, mouth, pores and other orifices. Then, if the man has a strong constitution, nature can expel the poison through ulcers, and if the ulcers putrefy, are strangled and fully run their course, the patient will be saved, as can be clearly seen. But if the poison should be stronger than his nature, so that his constitution cannot prevail against it, then the poison instantly lays siege to the heart and the patient dies within a short time, without the relief that comes from the formation of ulcers."

Finally, writing from Avignon, Louis Heyligen noted, "It is said that the plague takes three forms. In the first people suffer an infection of the lungs, which leads to breathing difficulties. Whoever has this corruption or contamination to any extent cannot escape but will die within two days. Another form...in which boils erupt under the armpits...a third form in which people of both sexes are attacked in the groin."

The Plague of Justinian

Given the lack of knowledge concerning disease and contagion, some writers inevitably claimed that the plague was brought down upon people by God. The Byzantine historian Procopius (ca. 500-565) insisted, "During these times there was a pestilence, by which the whole human race came near to being annihilated. Now in the case of all other scourges sent from heaven some explanation of a cause might be given by daring men, such as the many theories propounded by those clever in these matters, for they love to conjure up causes which are utterly incomprehensible to man…But for this calamity, it is quite impossible either to express in words or to conceive in thought any explanation, except indeed to refer it to God."[9]

The people across the empire may well have wondered what crimes they had committed to deserve such execrable tortures, and many may have been mindful of a religious controversy threatening to split the empire. The official religion of the state, Christianity, adhered to the teachings of Nicaea's ecclesiastical councils (325) and Chalcedon (451), which held that God was Trinity (the Father, the Son, and the Holy Spirit), equally sharing one divine nature. Furthermore, God the Son assumed a human nature without abandoning his divine nature. Discussions on the nature of God and Jesus Christ preoccupied the minds and hearts of the bishops and theologians, and they frequently fell out over them. Today, such disputes, which often turned on the interpretation of texts and nuances of meaning, may seem trivial, but to those living in an age of faith, the debates assumed vital importance. In Justinian's time, many of the bishops in Syria and Egypt maintained that when God became human in Jesus Christ, the two natures fused to become something unique. This idea was anathema to the orthodox bishops, and especially to the Bishops (Popes) of Rome, who were regarded as the successors of Peter, the Prince of the Apostles and held the most important position in the Christian Church.[10]

---

[9] Rosen 2008:217
[10] Justinian I 2009

Justinian was a Nicaea-Chalcedonian Christian, while his wife, Empress Theodora, sympathized with the Monophysites, giving shelter to Monophysite leaders such as Patriarch Severus of Antioch and Patriarch Anthimus of Constantinople in the imperial palace. When Pope Silverius insisted on upholding the excommunication of Anthimus that had been pronounced by his predecessor, Theodora sent General Belisarius to depose him.

A contemporary mosaic depicting Theodora

Theodora was a remarkable woman who elicited strong opinions for her and against her. Her family came from Cyprus, and she was the daughter of a bear trainer and an actress, hardly the kind of background that would lead a woman to an elite status. She followed in her mother's profession, and when she was just 16, she became the mistress of the governor of Pentapolis in Libya. Thereafter, she mixed in elite circles, even journeying to the imperial court in Constantinople, where she caught the eye of Justinian, who was then the heir to the throne. The future emperor wished to marry her, but Roman law forbade anyone of senatorial rank or higher from marrying an actress, an occupation widely associated with prostitution. Justinian's uncle, Emperor Justin I, repealed the law to allow the two to marry in 525, and from that point forward, Justinian regarded his wife as his partner in government as in everything else, even according her an imperial court in her own right.

Theodora was a powerful woman who was certainly difficult to control, but Justinian was prepared to tolerate Monophysitism for his own reasons. He could not afford to lose Egypt and Syria, both of which were economically vital to the empire, yet he also wanted to avoid alienating the Bishop of Rome and churches in the West. Thus, he wished to present himself as the champion of orthodoxy and attempted to bring about a reconciliation between the established orthodoxy and Monophysitism. To this end, he engineered the election of Bishop Vigilius of Rome (r. 537-555), who was expected to be an imperial puppet. Much to his dismay, Vigilius quickly took the Nicaea-Chalcedonian side, leaving the Church as divided as ever.

Regardless of the reasons, plenty of people across the Byzantine Empire viewed these maneuvers as an attempt by Justinian to impose religious uniformity with the "wrong" religion, backed by a strong and powerful empress. That Justinian did not personally share his wife's unorthodox beliefs were either unknown or deemed of little consequence, because those with no understanding of theological nuances simply considered her a heretic, and they believed she was attempting to pervert her husband and the empire. Doubtless, that was why God was afflicting them.

As a result, it should come as little surprise that the Plague of Justinian, named after the famous emperor himself, was widely blamed on the actions of the empire's leader. When the plague broke out in 541, the 60-year-old Justinian had reconquered North Africa and most of Italy, and along with those conquests, he could brag of the codification of Roman law in his *Corpus Juris Civilis* and an extensive building program which included the Hagia Sophia and public works such as hospitals. He had also strengthened trade and reformed administration. Certainly, he believed he deserved the adulation of his subjects – when he viewed the completed Hagia Sophia, he reportedly stated, "Solomon, I have outdone you."

Despite all those accomplishments, many held him in contempt if the historian Procopius is to be believed. According to Procopius, Justinian presided over a profoundly non-Christian and non-Roman regime. His famous work *Anecdota* (more widely known as *The Secret History*), written several years after the plague, levels a number of charges against the emperor and his government. In Procopius's eyes, the so-called glorious reconquests caused untold devastation and suffering, reducing the empire's subjects to misery and the imperial soldiers' status to something resembling slavery. In the imperial heartlands, the government was corrupt, and the people were oppressed. Religion was used as a tool of government tyranny, individuals were arrested, tortured, and killed without charges or trials, and critics of the regime disappeared without a trace. Procopius quite vividly condemned Justinian:

> "[H]is character was something I could not fully describe. For he was at once villainous and amenable; as people say colloquially, a moron. He was never truthful with anyone, but always guileful in what he said and did, yet easily hoodwinked by any who wanted to

deceive him. His nature was an unnatural mixture of folly and wickedness. What in olden times a peripatetic philosopher said was also true of him, that opposite qualities combine in a man as in the mixing of colors [sic]. I will try to portray him, however, insofar as I can fathom his complexity.

"This Emperor, then, was deceitful, devious, false, hypocritical, two-faced, cruel, skilled in dissembling his thought, never moved to tears by either joy or pain, though he could summon them artfully at will when the occasion demanded, a liar always, not only offhand, but in writing, and when he swore sacred oaths to his subjects in their very hearing. Then he would immediately break his agreements and pledges, like the vilest of slaves, whom indeed only the fear of torture drives to confess their perjury. A faithless friend, he was a treacherous enemy, insane for murder and plunder, quarrelsome and revolutionary, easily led to anything evil, but never willing to listen to good counsel, quick to plan mischief and carry it out, but finding even the hearing of anything good distasteful to his ears."11

The historian's assessment is so acrid that he claimed Justinian was possessed by a demon: "And some of those who have been with Justinian at the palace late at night, men who were pure of spirit, have thought they saw a strange demoniac form taking his place. One man said that the Emperor suddenly rose from his throne and walked about, and indeed he was never wont to remain sitting for long, and immediately Justinian's head vanished, while the rest of his body seemed to ebb and flow; whereat the beholder stood aghast and fearful, wondering if his eyes were deceiving him. But presently he perceived the vanished head filling out and joining the body again as strangely as it had left it."12

Indeed, the invective was not confined to Justinian. Empress Theodora, characterized as a sinister partner on a corrupt throne, was portrayed as a vulgar, shameless, and intensely political woman. *The Secret History* offers absolutely no deference to imperial dignity in its description of her: "Often, even in the theatre, in the sight of all the people, she removed her costume and stood nude in their midst, except for a girdle about the groin: not that she was abashed at revealing that, too, to the audience, but because there was a law against appearing altogether naked on the stage, without at least this much of a fig-leaf. Covered thus with a ribbon, she would sink down to the stage floor and recline on her back. Slaves to whom the duty was entrusted would then scatter grains of barley from above into the calyx of this passion flower, whence geese, trained for the purpose, would next pick the grains one by one with their bills and eat."13

In Procopius's opinion, Theodora was a demon in human form. He provided the following story: "Furthermore some of Theodora's lovers, while she was on the stage, say that at night a

---

11 Prokopios 2010: 8
12 Procopius 2010: 12.20–22
13 Procopius 2010: 12.20–22

demon would sometimes descend upon them and drive them from the room, so that it might spend the night with her. And there was a certain dancer named Macedonia, who belonged to the Blue [P]arty[14] in Antioch, who came to possess much influence. For she used to write letters to Justinian while Justin was still [e]mperor, and so made away with whatever notable men in the [e]ast she had a grudge against, and had their property confiscated."[15]

Procopius's account of Justinian, Theodora, and to a lesser extent Belisarius's misrule is questionable, given that no history is ever completely objective, but his sentiments were shared by other contemporary writers. For example, John of Ephesus, a Monophysite cleric, wrote that Theodora "came from a brothel," a strange claim to make of the patroness of the Monophysites if it was not widely believed.[16]

Certainly, both Theodora and her husband earned widespread opprobrium on account of their conduct during the Nika Riots in 532, which quickly escalated into a full-scale rebellion against the emperor. The people forcibly took Hypatius, an aristocrat and nephew of former emperor Anastasius I, and proclaimed him emperor. Justinian and his government were preparing to leave Constantinople when Theodora intervened, famously declaring it was better to die than flee, and that "royal purple is the noblest shroud."[17] Spurred on by his wife, Justinian ordered his generals, Belisarius and Mundus, to fall upon the rebels. Over 30,000 people reportedly perished, including the hapless Hypatius, who had had to be dragged to his coronation.

---

[14] The Blue Party was a political lobby associated with racing events at the Hippodrome.
[15] Procopius 2010: 12
[16] Prokopios 2010: xlix
[17] *Lend Me Your Ears* 1992: 37

A contemporary mosaic believed to depict Belisarius

The revolt was quelled, but not before there had been considerable destruction of the city's monumental core. In the four days between the beginning and the end of the uprising - from January 14 to January 18 - fires started by the rioters burned out of control. The buildings destroyed included the old Hagia Sophia (completed in 360 and remodeled in 415 under Theodosius II) and its neighbor Hagia Eirene, as well as the Augusteion, the Senate House, the Chalke Gate, the Baths of Zeuxippos, the great porticoes leading from the Severan core to the Forum of Constantine, and a large swath of buildings on either side of the Mese.

Excavated remains of Theodosius II's Hagia Sophia

Constantinople underwent one of its most important phases of urban development in response to the Nika riots. With so much of the capital's monumental core burned to the ground, Justinian undertook its restoration and rebuilding, and Procopius, the court historian of Justinian, wrote that the first project for reconstruction in the emperor's renewal of the capital was the new Hagia Sophia. He also lists other churches and then turns his attention to civic projects, which included the Great Palace and the Chalke Gate, the Augusteion and its Senta, the Baths of Zeuxippos, and the porticoes along the Mese. An enormous cistern, the Yerebatan Sarayi, was constructed under the Basilica.

Justinian's revitalization was spurred by the destruction that had taken place in the city, but he made it so comprehensive that it was necessary to extend all areas within the city's walls, as well as to the suburbs beyond them and the islands and territories up the Bosphorus. At the same time, while the project was obviously extensive and expensive, it did not transform the basic structure of the city because Justinian didn't establish any new civic projects like those that characterized the reigns of Constantine and Theodosius. The armature laid down by Constantine in the 320s and 330s remained the framework in which Justinian's project were constructed.

One major distinction that separated Justinian's projects from those of Constantine and Theodosius's campaigns, however, was the emphasis on religion. Much less civic construction was undertaken than was construction of religious institutions, which constituted a radical reversal from previous imperial urban renewal campaigns. Usually, efforts were directed at the development of civic spaces and institutions. In the city under Constantine, there were six religious foundations divided equally between pagan and Christian. By the time of Theodosius, it seems that the pagan churches had ceased to exist (probably due to suppression during the late 4th century purges of Hellenic cults), while the number of Christian churches had increased to 14. A century later, when Procopius was writing *The Buildings*, the number had already increased to 50. Thus, even though the urban form remained the same, the ethos had changed: Constantinople had changed from the embodiment of Roman ideals of civic splendor to a Christian city par excellence.

In his reconstruction efforts, Justinian employed an ambivalent approach to the Classical heritage of the city. In some places and buildings, Justinian placed old pagan statues from other parts of the city or from other places, such as Athens. However, as his reign progressed, he increasingly declined the use of public sculpture and the presence of antiquities, indicating that the antique world was no longer the cultural heart and soul of Constantinople, even if they had been under Constantine and Theodosius.

While these efforts undoubtedly improved the city, they are also evidence that Justinian and Theodora took great pains to emphasize their authority and quasi-divine power, commanding even the highest court dignitaries to prostrate themselves when in their presence. Nobody was permitted to address the sovereigns unless invited to do so, and a minutiae of court ceremonial procedures ensured the nobility were held captive to their thrall. In the words of Procopius, Justinian and Theodora "compelled everyone to dance attendance upon them like slaves."[18]

Given his intense dislike of the emperor, it is no surprise that Procopius found a way to attribute the evils of the pestilence to Justinian,[19] who, if not a demon in human form, had brought God's anger upon the people due to his crimes and irreverence. Other 6th century writers made the same accusations, but most adhered to the state propaganda by portraying Justinian and Theodora as sainted monarchs. The contemporaries who despised the emperor may have been happy to hear reports that even he contracted the plague in 541, despite the incense burners surrounding him in the imperial palace placed there to purge the air.

If such news gladdened those who shared Justinian's contempt of Procopius, then Theodora's appointment as regent must have concerned them. She now had full control of the government, and if the emperor died, which seemed inevitable, she could be counted on to groom a successor to do her bidding. Contemporary writers portrayed Empress Theodora as scheming,

---

[18] Prokopios 2010: XXX 30-31
[19] Prokopios 2010: XVIII 36-44

manipulative, and controlling Justinian, not simply supporting him. Powerful women were often described similarly throughout history, so it is difficult to get a fully objective sense of her personality, but it's clear she was fully aware of her abilities and was never shy about exercising her power. Anyone opposing her or attracting her suspicion was removed from power and destroyed.

When her husband was stricken with the plague, she ruled alone and found herself in a most precarious and vulnerable position. At the time, it was not clear that anyone could recover after coming down with the plague, and if Justinian died, Theodora's only chance of survival was to marry a nobleman acceptable to both the imperial Senate and herself.

At the same time, she first had to remove potential rivals to the throne. Theodora viewed General Belisarius as just such a rival, which made sense given that the legendary military leader was Master of the Troops (*Magister Militum*), which made him the most powerful nobleman. He was popular as the hero of the Vandal and Ostrogoth Wars and played a decisive role in restoring the empire's glory. Generally regarded by historians as one of the greatest military tacticians of all time, he was benevolent toward his soldiers and popular with the people. On the field, he was cautious and calculating, striking when the enemy was at its most vulnerable. It was probably an assessment of these qualities that convinced Theodora he would make a move on the imperial throne.

The empress's success in removing rivals had been demonstrated with the downfall of John of Cappadocia (not to be confused with the patriarch of Constantinople who died in 520). As Praetorian Prefect of the East, John of Cappadocia administered the imperial heartlands from the Danube to the Euphrates and the Nile, making him one of the most powerful men in the empire. He was a rival for influence with the emperor, which made him a danger to Theodora. Using Antonina, Belisarius's wife, she tricked him into declaring his treasonous intentions toward Justinian, after which he was stripped of his office and wealth and forced to take holy orders.

Like Theodora, Antonina had been an actress, dancer, and probable courtesan, and Belisarius had taken advantage of the same change of law that allowed Theodora to marry Justinian. Perhaps it was this shared background that served to make the empress and Antonina political allies. Antonina was, however, devoted to her husband, if not affectionately (she had an affair with Theodosius, one of her husband's aides), then politically, for she calculated that he had a better chance of succeeding to the throne if the emperor died. Thus, when Justinian was on what everyone believed was his deathbed, the empress did not share her thoughts with Antonina. Instead, she conducted an investigation into Antonina and Belisarius's intentions.

Over time, Theodora learned that Belisarius and his second-in-command, Bouzes, were openly discussing the succession and had reportedly sworn to oppose any of Theodora's candidates. Belisarius was too powerful to lay hands-on, but Bouzes was summoned to give an account of himself. What happened next was relayed by Procopius: "[Theodora] called Bouzes suddenly into the woman's apartment as if to communicate to him something very important. Now there was a suite of rooms in the Palace, below the ground level, secure and a veritable labyrinth, so that it seemed to resemble Tartarus, where she usually kept in confinement those who had given offence. So Bouzes was hurled into this pit, and in that place he, a man sprung from a line of consuls, remained, forever unaware of time. For as he sat there in the darkness, he could [not] distinguish whether it was day or night, nor could he communicate with any other person. For the man who threw him his food for each day met him in silence, one as dumb as the other, as one beast meets another. And straightway it was supposed by all that he had died, but no one dared mention or recall him. But two years and four months later she was moved to pity and released the man, and he was seen by all as one who had returned from the dead. But thereafter he always suffered from weak sight and his whole body was sickly."20

This sent a clear message to Belisarius and his allies, and Theodora moved against the general himself by relieving him of his command and confiscating his property. She did not have sufficient evidence to accuse him of treason, and he was almost certainly too popular to imprison or execute, but Belisarius must have feared for his life, figuring that Theodora would eventually find or manufacture a pretext to execute him.

Then, seemingly miraculously, the emperor recovered. It is extraordinarily rare for an individual to recover from the plague without treatment, and even today, doctors do not understand how recovery occurs. To the people of the empire, it must have seemed that God had performed a wonder by restoring their emperor to them. Both Theodora and Belisarius, who was restored to his rank, were understandably grateful for the divine intervention. Justinian himself might have imagined that God had thus set the seal on everything his reign had accomplished.

The plague also began to lift from the empire's ravaged cities and villages, and outbreaks became less frequent. Though the Byzantines could not know it, the plague was essentially burning itself out by running out of victims. No treatment had destroyed it, and epidemics that were more localized and less virulent would continue to ravage portions of Europe for the next 200 years, but as the spring of 542 neared, the people had a respite in which to assess the damage the calamity had caused.

Scholars estimate the pestilence killed between 25-50 million people, which represents 13-26% of Europe's population.[21] As a comparison, the Black Death of 1347-1351 took 30-60%,[22] though it should be kept in mind that this plague only lasted about four months, thus vastly outpacing the Black Death in terms of its deadly intensity.

One of the more immediate effects of the calamity was a phenomenal rise in the price of grain due to the plummeting of production in rural areas. The imperial treasure's reserves might have

---

[20] Prokopios 2010
[21] Rosen 2008: 3
[22] Austin Alchon 2003: 21

alleviated the shortage, but they had been invested in the military and public works. Moreover, Justinian insisted on collecting taxes, even from the estates of the dead, for state revenue had dropped profoundly and the courts were awash with inheritance lawsuits to the extent that legislation was enacted to limit them.

The pestilence decimated the military, and Justinian and Belisarius's conquests in Italy were immediately imperiled. The Goths, who had been reduced to northern Italy and cut off from Roman ports, suffered less from the plague and were thus able to overwhelm the weakened Byzantine presence. Moreover, Belisarius had been transferred east in response to an attack by the Persians.

By 545, the Gothic leader Totila had recovered most of Italy, including Rome, leaving the Byzantines with Sicily. In 551, the Byzantines invaded the area again and defeated the Goths at the Battle of Mons Lactarius (Vesuvius), and for the time being, Italy was reintegrated into Justinian's empire.

The victory was a somewhat hollow one because it cost the empire a lot of men and money, and the Byzantines did not have the means to adequately garrison occupied territories. In fact, there were only 16,000 troops assigned to Italy, and the entire cost of the reconquest was 137,000 kilograms of gold. In the east, the war with Persia was lost, and Justinian was forced to pay over 900 kilograms of gold annually in tribute to the Shah of Persia. The Rus from Kiev and the Turkic peoples who dwelled in the southern Steppes were raiding the lands south of the Danube. In 559, they descended upon Constantinople, where they were repulsed by Belisarius.

In 551, the same year the Byzantines won the Battle of Mons Lactarius, a severe earthquake shook the eastern Mediterranean, with its effects felt as widely as Alexandria and Antioch. It killed 30,000 people and triggered a tsunami that took many more. In the years ahead, the people might very well have viewed the calamity as an omen of the decline of imperial splendor.

The Roman Plague of 590

In 552, Justinian captured Cartagena and other Visigothic cities in southern Spain, as well as some territory in Africa south of the Strait of Gibraltar, but by the time the emperor died in 565 at the age of 83, he left the empire impoverished and weak, having only partially succeeded in restoring the grandeur of the Roman Empire. In struggling to maintain what gains he had made, he had left his people diminished and vulnerable. What money the treasury possessed was used to bribe the barbarians threatening to wreak havoc across the empire. Even the religious question remained unresolved, as Church leaders in the West continued resisting attempts to reconcile with the Monophysites, who themselves still regarded the emperor's efforts with deep suspicion. Theodora's premature death in 548, possibly of cancer, struck Justinian hard, and the failures of his later reign have been attributed to the lack of her guidance and steady hand.[23]

As if all that wasn't enough, Justinian had not succeeded in producing an heir, so his nephew followed him as Emperor Justin II. The new emperor, by his own admission proud, arrogant, and ill-counselled, was incapable of reversing the decline, and in 568, barely three years after Justinian's death, a new terror descended upon Italy after 14 years of fragile peace under Byzantine rule. The Lombards, a Germanic group originally from Scandinavia, crossed into Italy from Pannonia (roughly Austria), where they had been defending the empire's borders on the imperial payroll. The invasion of some 150,000 Lombards caught the Byzantines by surprise, and their smaller forces were swiftly overwhelmed by the Lombards, led by King Alboin. Four years later, Pavia, in north-central Italy, was captured and made the capital of the new Lombard kingdom. The region is still called Lombardy to this day.

The Ostrogoths had preserved Roman institutions when they took over Italy in 476 and used those vestiges to acquire and maintain legitimacy. Indeed, Odoacer, the first Gothic king of Italy, acknowledged the (purely nominal) sovereignty of the emperor in Constantinople. Conversely, the Lombards had no such respect and violently replaced the former culture with their own. Moreover, they did not adopt the religion of the population as other barbarians had, instead adhering either to pagan practices or Arian Christianity (in the 4th century, the priest Arius had taught that God the Son was not equal with God the Father, but that He was created by the latter).

Italy was divided between the great chieftains, with the Kingdom of Lombardy in the north and a number of duchies in the south. The imperial garrisons receded to the coastal fortresses and the regions surrounding them, where they could be supplied by sea. The principal of these was Ravenna, the capital on the eastern coast, followed by a region called Pentapolis ("five cities", corresponding to the Marches in modern Italy), and Rome, supplied by its port, Ostia. The two cities were joined by a territorial corridor through the easily defensible Apennine Mountains. The Byzantines also clung onto Liguria, Sicily, Corsica, Sardinia, Calabria, and southern Apulia.

The emperor's representative in Italy was the Exarch of Ravenna, and he was faced with the seemingly impossible task of defending his people against constant Lombard incursions as requests for help from Constantinople were almost always turned down. The emperors moved their troops and resources to Persia and the Danube on the eastern borders. The Avars had carved an empire for themselves from the Volga to the mountains of Bohemia and were pressing relentlessly into Thrace. Defending Constantinople from the Avar barbarians and the rich eastern provinces from the Persians were bigger priorities, so the Byzantines in Italy would have to defend themselves the best they could.

The exarch could exercise little influence beyond Ravenna, and in Rome especially, his authority was largely ignored. Ever since the reconquest of Rome in 536, the aristocracy was led by an imperial Senate in Rome, and they resented the appointment of Byzantine Greek governors

---

[23] Barker 1966: 191

over them. Thus, the exarch's representative in Rome, the Duke of Rome, exercised little effectual power.

In practice, the duke's functions were largely assumed by the Church and its bishop. When the imperial seat of power in the Western Roman Empire moved from Rome to Ravenna in the 5th century, the Bishop of Rome, already responsible for the care of widows, orphans, prisoners, and the poor, had taken up further civil responsibilities, including public health, weights and measures, and public entertainment. Ecclesiastical courts administered the law, for the Duchy of Rome ceased appointing judges. The Bishop of Rome thus provided for defending the populace against the Lombards' constant attacks, even recruiting troops for that purpose. Moreover, the Church was the richest and largest landowner in Italy, with estates in all of imperial-held Italy, including Sicily, Sardinia, Corsica, as well as southern Francia and North Africa. It may very well have been the largest landholder the entire Byzantine Empire. It seemed natural, then, that Italy would look to the Bishop of Rome more than any other Byzantine authority for defense.

This was the situation when a plague struck in 590. Byzantine authority in Italy had mostly collapsed before the onslaught of the Lombards, and Constantinople could not or would not assist, leading the Italian people to turn to the Church. This provided the origins of the Papal States, a unique entity that ruled much of central Italy until 1870. Modern Italy was also born there, for the Lombard invasion marked the first time that Italy had been politically divided. It would continue to be divided by several different states until the *Risorgimento* in the 19th century.

At the beginning of 590, the Bishop of Rome was Pelagius II, a man of Romano-Ostrogoth origin who had succeeded his predecessor, Benedict I, in 579, while the Lombards were besieging Rome. The Lombards would be his biggest concern for the entire length of his reign. The first act of his pontificate was to buy off the barbarians with gold, after which he petitioned Emperor Tiberius II (r. 574-582) for troops to defend the city. The request was refused, so Pelagius II urged Chilperic I (r. 539-584), the Catholic king of the Franks, for help. It would be the first of several requests from Rome to Francia rather than Constantinople, and Italy's destiny would soon be tied to that of Franks. On this occasion, however, the Franks invaded Italy but turned back after filling their purses with Lombard gold, so the Lombard assault continued.

More calamities would come. In the winter of 589, torrential rains caused the River Tiber to burst its banks, producing a catastrophic flood destroying many dwellings and churches. Most significantly, the flood destroyed the Church's granaries, which were necessary to feed the population in a state of almost constant siege. Stories circulated of monstrous serpents and dragons riding on the waters toward the port of Ostia and the sea. The violence of the floodwater and the debris it carried would have hampered shipping coming into the port, and it is likely that much-needed food and other supplies did not arrive by sea, at least not in sufficient quantities. With flooding, mud, the spread of filth and debris, hunger, and freezing temperatures, the conditions in Rome and the surrounding region (Latium) were ripe for a public health disaster.

The first signs of the plague appeared in Rome in January 590, as people began to suffer from fever, boils, gangrene, and horrific muscular pain. These were all too recognizable after the Plague of Justinian a less virulent outbreak in 543. There were probably not many people alive in Rome in 590 who had known past outbreaks within the city's walls, but historical records certainly existed, and the plague had occurred in various parts of Italy and Gaul since then. The pestilence had flared in Ostia in 570, but it was contained and did not spread to Rome, which was remarkable since the city was Rome's trading port. At the same time, Avignon and Viviers, both on the Rhone River and in southern Francia, were stricken, suggesting the contagion came from Frankish ports. If the medieval *Golden Legend,* a collection of the saints' lives written much later, is to be believed, the people thought the stench from rotting monsters caught up in the flood had caused the disease. They also saw the sky filled with arrows flying toward the city.

Bishop Gregory of Tours, writing of the plague as reported by a deacon living in Rome, described the horrific disease in apocalyptic terms by alluding to the prophet Ezekiel: "Utterly destroy old and young, maidens, children and women: but upon whomsoever you shall see the sign of the cross, kill him not, and begin ye at my sanctuary."[24] By "my sanctuary," Gregory of Tours meant the holy Church of Rome, particularly its head, Pelagius, who was one of the first victims of the plague. As the Bishop of Rome lay dying in the Lateran Palace surrounded by the chants of the clergy and offerings of incense for his speedy entrance into Heaven, the question of succession lay heavily on the minds of the Roman clergy and nobility. The successor would have to be a giant among men, someone who could deal with the suffering caused by the plague and the Lombards. Deacon Gregory seemed a natural choice, as his family was of senatorial rank, and he was the papal ambassador to Constantinople. As such, he would be acceptable to both the emperor (whose confirmation was still required at this point in time) and the Roman nobility. Moreover, he was a deeply pious man who would appeal to the people. Indeed, he was the abbot of Saint Andrew's monastery.

Gregory devoted his life to contemplation and peace, rebelled at his election, and wrote to Emperor Maurice (r. 582-602) to undo the result, but once the clergy and people let it be known that their decision was final, he set about the task of governing with resolution and energy. He immediately addressed the Roman people, urging them to do penance for their sins with prayer and fasting. Next, he personally led them in a procession through the churches of Rome to petition God to alleviate their suffering. The *Golden Legend* describes how the procession was led by an image of the Blessed Virgin Mary, and worshippers dropped to the ground, even as it wound through the streets. The people chanted invocations to God, the Virgin Mary, and the saints. Angelic voices sang:

"O Queen of Heaven, rejoice, alleluia,

---

[24] Ezekiel 9, 6.

For He whom thou didst merit to bear, alleluia,

hath arisen as he said, alleluia!"

To these words, the pious Gregory added, "Pray for us. O God, we beseech Thee!"[25]

As the supplicants approached the Mausoleum of Emperor Hadrian, they saw Archangel Michael, the heavenly spirit that cast the demons into hell, sheath his sword over the city, and the pestilence abated. Thereafter, the Mausoleum was referred to as the Castel Sant'Angelo. Visitors to Rome may see a statue of the archangel returning his sword to its scabbard on top of the ancient Roman fortress. Catholics continued to revere Saint Michael as a protector against the plague. This is evidenced by the inhabitants of Nativitas, Mexico, who claimed, in 1631, that he revealed a miraculous spring that healed them from smallpox.

Toby Jorgensen's picture of Castel Sant'Angelo

The miraculous elements in this account are easy to question, but the litany used for that procession is still in use in the Catholic Church today. The *Litaniae Sanctorum,* Litany of the Saints, continues to contain the petition, "From plague, famine and war, deliver us." This first prayerful solemnity survives in the form of Rogation Day (from the Latin word *rogare*, "to ask"), commemorated on April 25, the traditional date of Gregory's procession. The image of the

---

[25] Ryan 2012

mother of Jesus, a painting titled *Salus Populi Romani* (*Salvation of the Roman People*), also exists. It was transferred to Rome from Constantinople for the procession and was painted by the apostle Luke according to tradition. It is now in the Basilica of Saint Mary Major in Rome.

The efficacy of the Roman peoples' prayers may be debatable, but it can be appreciated that Gregory's leadership gave them courage and hope. The pestilence abated about five months later.

The extent of the misery caused by the plague in 590 is difficult to gauge due to a lack of documented evidence, but Rome had not been a great city for nearly 400 years by that time, and when the Western Roman Empire fell to the Ostrogoths in 476, Rome was already a minor city. The capital at the time was Ravenna, and Rome had been depopulated thanks to barbarian attacks and economic stress. Thus, the city's population, which had once been about 1.5 million people in the middle of the 1st century CE, had fallen to about 35,000 in the early 6th century.[26] If the plague in 590 took a third of Rome's population, then the once mighty capital might have been reduced to around 20,000 or less, taking into account the plague in 543 and the Lombard attacks. Rome would have been little more than a shell of its former self, with many great buildings and monuments such as the Forum and the Colosseum already wasting away due to the lack of manpower and funds. Public areas were given over to livestock, and commerce and manufacture, already on the decline, ground to a halt. Trade was practically nonexistent, and the once powerful nobility of the city was weak and reduced to begging along with the lower classes. Senators were little more than figureheads who turned to the Bishop of Rome for leadership.

Fortunately, Gregory possessed a character as powerful and energetic as the calamities afflicting his city, and he diverted grain from the ecclesiastical states in Sicily to feed his people. To deal with the Lombards, Gregory did what his predecessors had not dared: when the exarch failed to provide for the defence of the towns and cities, he appointed governors and military officers. He also concluded truces with the Lombards, which usually involved handing over gold.

These measures gave Italy periods of peace, but they infuriated the Byzantine emperor and exarch. To their remonstrations, he replied that if the rulers would not aid the ruled, then their subjects must fend for themselves. By the time Gregory died in 602, his actions advanced the Roman Church's temporal authority and laid the foundation of the Papal States. Inasmuch as the plague in 590 occasioned his election, it could be said that the Papal States owed their existence at least in part to that pestilence, though the Lombard incursions undoubtedly a stronger factor.

Precursor to the Black Death

The plagues of the 6th century represented the beginning of what historians and medical experts call the First Plague Pandemic, with the second beginning with the Black Death in 1350 and the

---

[26] Population 2020

third beginning in 1855 and ending around 1960. The plague was not entirely dormant between these major outbreaks, and even today, outbreaks of the plague occur, though, with medical technology and preventative measures, they are unlikely to assume the monstrous proportions of earlier years.

In 680, the plague returned to ravage Rome and much of northern Italy. The political situation in Italy had hardly changed at the time, but the rest of the empire was under assault by a new and potent force: the Muslims. Muhammad's religious movement had taken hold in Arabia and spilled into Africa, the Levant, and Asia Minor, and the Islamic caliphate began to come into conflict with the Byzantine Empire. Italy had been left to its own devices, and there was still no prospect of help. The Lombards had finally adopted Roman manners and culture and converted to Catholicism, but this seems to have done little to mitigate their hostility. The population of Rome had swollen due to an influx of refugees from the east and Frankish pilgrims who looked increasingly to Rome rather than Constantinople for guidance.

Most importantly, sanitation in the damp, low-lying city had not improved since 590. Paul the Deacon, a Lombard historian writing toward the end of the 8th century, claimed that several members of a family would be carried away from a house on the same bier and that people knew how many in a household died by the number of knocks an angel made on the door. In Rome, the plague even took the life of the Bishop of Rome, Agatho, who had previously been a monk. Michael.

Paul wrote of the desolation, "For the common report had it that those who fled would avoid the plague, the dwellings were left deserted by their inhabitants, and the dogs alone kept house. The flocks remained alone in the pastures with no shepherd at hand. You might see villages [villas] or fortified places lately filled with crowds of men, and on the next day all had departed and everything was in utter silence. Some fled, leaving the corpses of their parents unburied; parents forgetful of their duty abandoned their children in raging fever. If by chance long-standing affection constrained anyone to bury his near relative, he remained himself unburied, and while he was performing funeral rites he perished; while he offered obsequies to the dead, his own corpse remained without obsequies. You might see the world brought back to its ancient silence; no voice in the field, no whistling shepherds; no lying in wait of wild beasts among the cattle; no harm to domestic fowls. The crops, outliving the time of the harvest, awaited the reaper untouched; the vineyard with its fallen leaves and its shining grapes remained undisturbed while winter came on; a trumpet as of warriors resounded through the day and night; something like a murmur of an army was heard by many; there were no footsteps of passersby, no murderer was seen, yet corpses of the dead were more than the eye could discern; pastoral places had been turned into a desert, and human habitations had become places of refuge for wild beasts.[27]

In Pavia, the capital of the Lombard kingdom, streets were deserted as inhabitants fled to the

---

[27] Diaconus 1907: 2.4 {1}.

mountains to escape the plague. They were gone so long that grass and shrubbery took over the city. It was around this time that devotion to Saint Sebastian, a Roman soldier killed for his faith around 288, became popular. Sebastian was shot to death by arrows, and his association with the plague may come from myths surrounding the god Apollo, who fired the plague upon poor mortals in the form of arrows. In 680, the bones of Saint Sebastian were transferred to Pavia from Rome, and the pestilence abated around the same time.

The horrors of the plague were by no means confined to the Mediterranean. The plague arrived in the British Isles for the first time in 664, first appearing in Leinster, Ireland, or according to the English, the south of England. As with other outbreaks, historians recorded omens foretelling the calamity. Astronomers have confirmed that an eclipse occurred on May 1, 664. As for the earthquake that was reported, tremors have not been infrequently reported in the British Isles (an 1884 quake in Colchester damaged 1,200 buildings).[28]

The English called the epidemic *on-flyge* ("on-flying"), an apt description of the pace at which it spread. The plague spread everywhere across the British Isles save for a section of northern Scotland, ravaging the region for about 20 years. There remains some debate as to what kind of disease it was; earlier historians believed it was the Bubonic Plague, probably transmitted through trade on the continent, but some modern scholars think smallpox is the likely culprit.[29]

The plague also struck Ctesiphon on the eastern bank of the Tigris, Persia in 628, slaying more than 100,000 people, and the Muslim world was afflicted for the first time in 638 when a large Arab army invading Byzantine-held Syria was hit by the plague and lost about 25,000 men.[30] In 697, the pestilence returned to Constantinople before passing back into Egypt and Syria in 704, where it intermittently ravaged the population over the first half of the 8th century.

In 749, it visited Constantinople once more, and it did so much damage that according to the historian Nicephorus Byzantinus, it almost depopulated the city.[31] From there, it spread through Greece and the Aegean Islands, then returned to Italy. After that, the Bubonic Plague seems to have disappeared.

The effects of the pandemic are almost impossible to overstate. When it first struck in the middle of the 6th century, the Byzantine Empire under Justinian was on the verge of a new golden age. The emperor aimed to reunite the West and East and was on the cusp of achieving this goal. Italy and North Africa had been reconquered, and the Byzantines had also conquered part of Spain, even after the first outbreak. Historians can only wonder how the world might have turned out had Justinian or his successors captured all of Spain, conquered the Franks, or even recovered the British Isles. He certainly laid the foundations for doing so by reforming and

---

[28] Earthquakes 2020
[29] Kohn 2007: 449
[30] Simpson (2012): 18
[31] Simpson (2012): 18

reinvigorating both the imperial economy and the military. The Middle Ages, marked by the domination of Germanic kingdoms in Western Europe, might never have happened as they did, or they might have been delayed at least. Instead, a new Roman/Byzantine golden age might have enveloped the lands bordering the Mediterranean, and the Arab incursions in the 7th century might have been quelled.

However, when the plague affected the Byzantine Empire, the army was decimated and trade, agriculture, and revenues collapsed. Justinian's grand offensive was mostly abandoned, and the empire struggled merely to defend its borders. This occurred throughout various parts of the empire over the course of 200 years, and the imperial economy had no sizeable space from which to recover its misfortunes.

Meanwhile, the Franks, Goths, Lombards, and Saxons did not suffer from the plague as much, probably because their trade networks and military and political organizations were not as developed and complex. Ironically, that lack of sophistication allowed them to subsequently consolidate their rule in Western Europe. The Church, headed by the Bishop of Rome, looked increasingly to other kingdoms in Western Europe for protection, and it was the Franks rather than the emperors in Constantinople who delivered the Church from the Lombards in 774. When the Western Roman Empire was "restored" in 801, it was a joint Frankish-Roman creation, with Pope Leo III (r. 795-816) placing the crown on Charlemagne's head in an act that was a definitive break with the imperial east. The split of Christendom between the Eastern Orthodox Church and the Catholic Church and the emergence of modern Europe were complex affairs in which many unresolved issues played their part, but the Plague of Justinian and the outbreaks that followed were pivotal factors.[32]

Today, many wonder why the plague essentially stopped spreading and killing people in the mid-8th century, particularly since *Yersinia pestis* is one of the deadliest organisms evolution has ever produced. Incredibly, it may have actually been too deadly to destroy the human race, simply because it also kills the fleas that transmit it and the rats that the fleas live on. One source explains the gruesome way in which the plague kills fleas: "The bacteria multiply inside the flea, sticking together to form a plug that blocks its stomach and causes it to starve. The flea then bites a host and continues to feed, even though it cannot quell its hunger, and consequently the flea vomits blood tainted with the bacteria back into the bite wound. The Bubonic Plague bacterium then infects a new victim, and the flea eventually dies from starvation.[33] In other words, the plague killed all of its local hosts and carriers and thus could advance no further.

Some fascinating if macabre research done on victims of the Black Death in the 14th century indicates that the strain of *Y.pestis* was unlike any that exists today. DNA evidence has led experts to conclude that the Black Death just burned out, which strongly suggests that the Plague

---

[32] Kohn, p.218.
[33] Plague 2020

of Justinian was of a different strain, albeit one that was also too deadly to survive.[34]

It might also be asked why so little is known about the Plague of Justinian and the epidemics following it, which stands in stark contrast with the Black Death, which has been the subject of numerous books and papers. The explanation, at least in part, is probably cultural. The 300 years between the fall of the Western Roman Empire and its revival by the Franks has long been referred to as the Dark Ages, negatively comparing the cultural enlightenment of the Roman Empire with the supposed barbarity of the Germanic kingdoms that replaced it. This was popularized by the Romantic Movement in the 19th century[35] and was premised on the belief that Western Civilization was superior. In doing so, Western Europeans ignored the rich cultural traditions of the Byzantine Empire and Persia and overlooked that the Germanic peoples actually preserved some elements of Roman civilization. Moreover, tribes converting to Christianity embraced the Catholic Church and thus Roman culture. Contrary to popular opinion, learning did not decline during this time in the West because monasticism brought schools, libraries, and institutes of higher learning throughout Western Europe.

Now, historians are beginning to more fully appreciate that the Early Middle Ages was a fascinating period during which the ancient world was morphing into Europe as it is now known, bringing with it the knowledge, philosophy, and culture of the past and infusing everything with Christianity. In the same vein, historians are beginning to analyze the Plague of Justinian in a new light, and it is possible that new insights will be discovered as they analyze the plague's permanent political and religious ramifications.

Online Resources

Other books about the Byzantine Empire by Charles River Editors

Other books about the plague on Amazon

Further Reading

Austin Alchon, Suzanne (2003). *A Psest in the Land: New World Epidemics in a Global Perspective*. New Mexico: University of New Mexico Press.

Barker, John W. (1966). *Justinian and the later Roman Empire*. Wisconsin: University of Wisconsin Press.

Bazian. (2014). New Strains of the Black Death could emerge. *National Health Service*. https://www.nhs.uk/news/medical-practice/new-strains-of-the-black-death-could-emerge/

Diaconus, Paulus. (1907). *History of the Lombards* (William Dudley Foulke, Trans.).

---

[34] Salzberg 2011
[35] Mommsen 1942

Pennsylvania: University of Pennsylvania. http://www.thule-italia.org/Nordica/Paul%20the%20Deacon%20-%20History%20of%20the%20Lombards%20(1907)%20[EN].pdf.

Earthquakes in the U.K. (2020). *British Geological Survey.* https://www.bgs.ac.uk/discoveringGeology/hazards/earthquakes/UK.html.

Eroshenko, Galina A. (2017, October 26). *Yersinia pestis* strains of ancient phylogenetic branch 0.ANT are widely spread in the high-mountain plague foci of Kyrgyzstan. *Plos One, 12*(10).

Friedman, Hannah. (2007). Bryn Mawr Classical Review 2007.08.25: Plague and the End of Antiquity: The Pandemic of 541-750. *Bryn Mawr Classical Review.* http://bmcr.brynmawr.edu/2007/2007-08-25.html.

Harl, Kenneth W. (2015). Finances under Justinian. *Early Medieval and Byzantine Civilization: Constantine to Crusades.*

Justinian I. (2009). Novel 131: Concerning Ecclesiastical Canons and Privileges. *Annotated Justinian Code* (Fred H. Blume and Timothy Kearley, Eds.) (Fred H. Blume, Trans.) Laramie: University of Wyoming College of Law, http://www.uwyo.edu/lawlib/blume-justinian/ajc-edition-2/novels/121-140/novel%20131_replacement.pdf.

Kohn, George Childs. (2007). *Encyclopedia of Plague and Pestilence: From Ancient Times to the Present.* New York: Facts on File.

Mango, Cyril A. (1980). *Byzantium: The Empire of New Rome.* New York: Scribner.

Mommsen, T. (1942). Petrarch's Conception of the "Dark Ages". *Speculum, 17*(2), 226-242. doi:10.2307/2856364.

Plague. (2017). *World Health Organization.* https://www.who.int/news-room/fact-sheets/detail/plague.

Plague (2019). *Centers for Disease Control and Prevention.* https://www.cdc.gov/plague/maps/index.html.

Population of Rome over Time. (2020). *Jetpunk.* https://www.jetpunk.com/charts/population-of-rome-over-time.

Procopius. (1894). De Aedificiis, in *The Church of St. Sophia Constantinople* (W. Lethaby and H. Swainson, Trans.), pp. 24-28. New York.

Prokopios. (2010). *The Secret History* (Anthony Kaldellis, Trans.). Indianapolis: Hackett

Publishing.

Rosen, William Rosen. (2008). *Justinian's Flea: the First Great Plague and the End of the Roman Empire*. Manhatten: Random House.

Ryan, W., & Duffy, E. (2012). Saint Gregory. In *The Golden Legend: Readings on the Saints*. Princeton University Press. Retrieved from www.jstor.org/stable/j.ctt7stkm.51

Simpson, W. J. (2012). *A Treatise on Plague: Dealing with the Historical, Epidemiological, Clinical, Therapeutic and Preventive Aspects of the Disease (Cambridge Library Collection - History of Medicine)*. Cambridge: Cambridge University Press.

Lend Me Your Ears: Great Speeches in History (Safire, William, Ed.). (1992). New York: W.W. Norton.

The Black Death and Early Public Measures. (2020). Science Museum: Brought to Life, http://broughttolife.sciencemuseum.org.uk/broughttolife/themes/publichealth/blackdeath.

Plague (disease). (2020). *Wikipedia: The Free Encyclopedia.* https://en.wikipedia.org/wiki/Plague_(disease).

Salzberg, Steven. (2011). The Black Death is dead (thanks to evolution). *Forbes.* https://www.forbes.com/sites/stevensalzberg/2011/09/02/the-black-death-is-dead-thanks-to-evolution/#2f8b8a1a33d2.

Wagner, David M., et al. (2014). Yersinia pestis and the Plague of Justinian 541–543 A.D.: a Genomic Analysis. *The Lancet, 14(4).* https://www.thelancet.com/journals/laninf/article/PIIS1473-3099(13)70323-2/fulltext.

Wohletz, Ken. (2000). Were the Dark Ages Triggered by Volcano-Related Climate Changes in the 6th Century? *Los Alamos National Laboratory,* https://www.lanl.gov/orgs/ees/geodynamics/Wohletz/Krakatau.htm.

Free Books by Charles River Editors

We have brand new titles available for free most days of the week. To see which of our titles are currently free, click on this link.

Discounted Books by Charles River Editors

We have titles at a discount price of just 99 cents everyday. To see which of our titles are currently 99 cents, click on this link.

Made in the USA
Middletown, DE
24 October 2020